THE ALCHEMY OF COOKING

Rosenberry books, etc.

WIPF & STOCK • Eugene, Oregon

Foreword by Thomas Moore

It takes a brave person to write a cookbook these days, when everyone seems to have a strict and narrow moral code for what is acceptable, healthy and digestible. Dr Rosen, or in this case he may prefer his nom de comedy "Dr Nada," handles the problem deftly with simple alternatives. He skirts the food hysteria that has become part of life in the twenty-first century.

As I read this user-friendly cookbook, I became aware of certain underlying values that make the book appealing to me. It's the hysteria issue. In this book you will sense no heroics, no school-marmish admonitions about what you should eat, no depth interpretations, no spiritual fervor, no psychoanalytic parsing of dinner. What you get is a sophisticated man choosing to eat simply, and inviting, not even encouraging, others to share in his culinary happiness. Chef as therapist.

The recipes are basic, and the references to C. G. Jung spare but evocative. Studying them carefully, I was reminded of James Hillman's *Freud's Own Cookbook* with its recipes for such psychological fare as "Momovers" and "Paranoid Pie."

I am certain that this book is the humorous work of Dr Nada. When was the last time you bought a cookbook that tells you how to make a standard peanut butter and jelly sandwich? Now, when I need to look up a recipe for peanut butter and jelly, I know that I can turn to this slender volume. I'll find an imaginative approach that adds nothing, absolutely nothing, to the recipe any young child would normally employ after a long day at school. Except maybe that Dr Nada covers his two pieces of bread separately with the jelly and peanut butter and then slams them together.

The recipes here look good, but the way of life even better.

Also by David H. Rosen

Patient-Centered Medicine: A Human Experience (with Uyen Hoang)
Spelunking through Life
Living with Evergreens
In Search of the Hidden Pond
Less is More (edited with Carol Goodman)
Lost in the Long White Cloud: Finding My Way Home
Time, Love and Licorice: A Healing Coloring Storybook
Clouds and More Clouds
The Tao of Elvis (Rosenberry/Wipf & Stock editions)
The Healing Spirit of Haiku (with Joel Weishaus)
Evolution of the Psyche (with Michael Luebbert)
The Tao of Jung: The Way of Integrity
Transforming Depression: Healing the Soul through Creativity
Medicine as a Human Experience (with David Reiser)
Lesbianism: A Study of Female Homosexuality

Acknowledgments

The author expresses a heartfelt thanks to Lanara Sophia Emmanuel Rosen, who is an exceptional cook; and to Bonnie A. Sheehey for her consultation and editorial assistance. I also appreciate my nutritional chemist, Tara Palmer, and her suggestions for healthy eating. In addition, I thank my parents (Barbara and Max Rosen) for serving me good food as a child (despite the liver and onions, and tongue).

ISBN: 978-1-5326-3340-9

Designed by Rosenberry books, etc.
101 Nicks Bend West
Pittsboro, NC 27312
800.723.0336 919.969.2767
www.rosenberrybooks.com
Rosenberry books, etc. is a registered trademark.

Wipf & Stock is an imprint of Wipf and Stock Publishers.
199 W. 8th Ave., Suite 3
Eugene, OR 97401
wipfandstock.com

Preface

Is there really a need for another cookbook? Yes, but not just any cookbook. What you are holding in your hands is a unique but tiny — almost haiku-like — comedic and Jungian eatery text. It comes from rural Oregon, where innovation is a part of everyday life (we all know that Oregon has an impact on the country and world). As comedian "Dr Nada," I spike the cookbook with humor. As Dr Rosen, Jungian analyst, I relish a bit of al dente wisdom along with the nourishing comfort food. Jung loved to cook, and I recall seeing his recipes in his lived-in kitchen at Bollingen.

The Alchemy of Cooking meets the demand for individuals who cannot eat sugar, gluten and dairy. I have lived and eaten in many nations, and like our great country, this cookbook is a melting pot of delicious things. At the same time, most items can be grown or obtained locally and inexpensively. For example, tonight I will have locally grown vegetables (Swiss chard and broccoli) with fish from the nearby Pacific ocean.

The Alchemy of Cooking follows the classic three meals a day, but allows for snacks in between and late at night. While often vegetarian, you will find meat sometimes an option. This cookbook will be especially useful for single men: many of the recipes I cooked for my three daughters after a divorce.

We thank the Supreme Being for loving to eat! It is my hope that more people will munch wisely, and spend less at the grocery store. Indeed, why not buy seeds and grow as much as you can? That's how we all started: with a family garden and farm. I recommend everything organic and also encourage going to your local farmer's market. Eat seasonal fruits and veggies. If not in season, you can always purchase fresh frozen.

I am fortunate to live with one of the best cooks in the world, Lanara Rosen. She is my mentor and model for *The Alchemy of Cooking*.

So, come on the Oregon trail, enjoy these meals
and some archetypal laughter.

David H. Rosen
Eugene, Oregon

Laughter is highest where food is best.
Irish Proverb

THE ALCHEMY OF COOKING

recipes with a

Jungian Twist

David H. Rosen

art by Diane Katz

All happiness depends on a leisurely breakfast.
John Gunther

BREAKFAST

Every meal is important, but how you start the day is critical. Just imagine your stomach being hit with a drive-thru sausage and egg sandwich and then dowsed with mediocre coffee. Reflect on how you get up in the morning. What do you usually do? Many people look out the window to see what kind of day it's going to be. Now I ask you to imagine your mouth, esophagus and stomach waiting for wholesome and tasty food. You are what you eat. Treat your stomach as your best friend. Even if it's a fast break, take your time and enjoy it. Remember, your tummy wants to smile and laugh.

Celebrate the dawn with a sunrise breakfast.

Anima Eggs and Animus Veggies or Bacon
(2-4 servings)

While you prepare the eggs, get the juice ready. If you want to get an immediate thanks, serve a glass of fresh squeezed orange juice. It's also fitting to cut a grapefruit in half and then into segments. Or, I love ruby red grapefruit juice.

Cook the eggs in one of the traditional ways: boiled (soft, medium or hard), fried or scrambled. After a bad night, you might feel scrambled, so the last option is the one you want.

Chop asparagus or your choice of vegetable. Cook chopped fresh veggies in coconut oil.

Cook the bacon crisp, or medium, if you insist. For a change, try the bacon from the country up north. However, remember it's important to cook it through.

If you want bacon, go for it, but bless the pigs that are sacrificed. I feel the same way about vegetables. I say a prayer to the green goddess Nature before eating them.

Get the coffee going. Espresso is a favorite. If you don't like something that strong, make a regular cup of Joe or a healthier beverage, such as green tea.

While you are cooking, don't hesitate to put on some music that defines America, like Hank Williams's "Say hey, good lookin' whatcha got cookin'?"

Homemade granola (serves 6)

1/2 cup chopped dates or dried figs	1/4 cup chopped pecans
	1/8 cup coconut oil
1/4 cup pumpkin seeds	1/3 cup raisins
1/2 cup water	1/8 cup apple juice
1/3 cup sliced almonds	1/4 cup sunflower seeds
3 cups gluten-free rolled oats	1/8 cup maple syrup
2/3 cup shredded coconut	1/8 cup sesame seeds

A tincture of hope

Preheat oven to 350 degrees F. Combine water and dates in a saucepan over medium heat to form a sticky paste.

Combine the remaining ingredients in a large bowl and mix. Spread the mixture flat on a large baking sheet. Bake for 7 minutes.

Remove baking sheet from oven. Mix granola with the sticky paste. Bake for 6 more minutes and let cool before enjoying.

Serve in cereal bowl and top it off with seasonal fruit such as blueberries, peaches, strawberries, or apricots. Add almond milk. On a special occasion, use coconut yogurt, which is made from coconut cream ... you won't be sorry!

Store leftover granola in a sealed container, or use for a nice midday or late night snack. Hey, that's why we made this granola for six servings!

When romantic love turns to oatmeal love,
this is a perfect day starter.

Oatmeal (4 servings)

2 cups rolled or steel-cut oats
3 1/2 cups water
Fresh fruit or dried fruit
Coconut or agave nectar

In a medium saucepan, bring water to boil.

Add oats and let simmer, uncovered, for 5 minutes, stirring occasionally. Remove pan from heat.

Serve in bowls with fresh cut fruit and drizzle with coconut or agave nectar to taste. And, if you want a continuing friendship, serve with coconut yogurt.

One of the very nicest things about life is the way we must regularly stop whatever it is we are doing and devote our attention to eating.
Luciano Pavorotti & William Wright

Individuated Omelette (2-4 servings)

It feels and tastes like love.

4-6 eggs
3 to 5 sliced mushrooms
1 to 2 sliced red or green bell pepper
1/2 cup spinach, finely chopped
   (substitute kale or Swiss chard)
1/2 cup chopped lean ham or tempeh

In a large saucepan, saute veggies in coconut oil over medium heat. To that, add chopped ham or tempeh.

Beat eggs (if angry) and add to the saucepan.

Cook eggs through and fold omelette in half.

Cut omelette and serve with a fresh parsley sprig or a bed of fresh basil.

Food for thought is no substitute
for the real thing.
Walt Kelly

If you've come this far searching for something easy, then you'll like what follows.

Toast & Fruit (2 servings)
quickest of all

Gluten free bread with coconut oil butter substitute (if you like, organic peanut butter or tasty almond butter).

You may protest: But, we can't eat toast without something like butter. Please try it for a week and then attempt to go back to butter. At restaurants we always eat butter, but then we go to confession.

Enjoy half of a grapefruit, sliced apple, pear, orange, or even kiwi. Make it tropical by serving fresh cantaloupe, honeydew or watermelon. It's a small world after all.

I think of W.C. Fields who said, "I never drink water. I'm afraid it will be habit forming." Hey no worries, I prefer and recommend the shadow drink — coffee that looks and tastes like the black sun. Let's remember that one cup of java is anti-inflammatory.

Eat and take a siesta —
even on the carpet under your desk.
Dr Nada

LUNCH

Avocado Delight (2 servings)

1 large ripe avocado
healthy organic gluten-free crackers (I recommend Jilz)
salami slices (optional)
kombucha or favorite juice
    (wine or beer, if you're off work)

Sorry Coke and Pepsi, but I don't recommend sugar-loaded soft drinks. In fact, the reader will note that up to this point, I have never mentioned sugar at all.

Slice avocado in half and remove the seed.

Have olive oil and balsamic vinegar available, as they go well with the avocado (or use a bit of of your favorite dressing).

Serve with crackers and salami slices.

Strange to see how a good dinner
and feasting reconciles everybody.
The Diary of Samuel Pepys

Veggie Salad (2-4 servings)

4 to 6 cups fresh spinach or arugula
1 to 2 chopped tomatoes
1 to 2 cups drained organic black beans
1/2 sliced avocado
1/4 cup seedless black olives
1/8 cup pumpkin seeds (optional but tasty)
1/8 cup blueberries
   (optional and delicious … also rich in antioxidants)

If you need directions for this, you probably need an appointment with Dr Nada or another comedic doctor. However, for those who insist, here they are:

Wash vegetables first, mix ingredients and serve or store in sealed container.

Add olive oil and vinegar when ready to eat.

Quickest of all

Grab a small yogurt container of your favorite flavor, along with a Raw Revolution, or other grain bar of your choice, and a piece of fruit (apple, pear, banana).

With a komboucha, this will be a fortifying and very rapid lunch.

Peanut/Almond Butter & Jelly Sandwich
(2 servings)

Probably Freud didn't indulge in this, but I imagine Jung did! After all, he formulated active imagination.

Freshly made gluten-free bread
1 jar peanut or almond butter
1 jar of your favorite jelly
    (we like grape and black raspberry — they both have antioxidants). Of course a sugar-free jelly is best and highly recommended. Everything is better without sugar, as it is associated with depression and inflammation.

Spread peanut or almond butter on one slice of bread. Then put the jelly on the other slice.

Think back to your childhood and enjoy with an apple! As an older person, I enjoy organic prunes.

Be thankful, however, that I did not recommend bologna sandwiches. This is where Jung was right: reflect on your best moments, not those painful experiences.

Vegetable Soup (4 servings)

When divorced and cooking for my daughters,
this was a favorite.

2 tbsp olive oil
1/4 tsp black pepper, freshly ground
1 cup leeks, finely chopped
1 cup fresh green beans, chopped
1 tbsp garlic, finely-minced
2 cups chopped tomatoes
1 tsp lemon juice, freshly squeezed
1 cup potatoes, peeled and diced
1 ear corn, kernels removed, or small can
1 quart vegetable or chicken broth
1/8 cup fresh parsley, chopped
1 cup carrots, peeled and chopped

Heat the olive oil in large pot over medium-low heat. Once hot, add leeks, garlic and a pinch of salt. Cook until soft, around 10 minutes. Add carrots, potatoes, green beans and continue to cook for another 7 minutes, stirring occasionally.

Add the stock, increase the heat to high, and bring to a simmer. Add the tomatoes, corn, and pepper. Reduce heat to low. Cover and cook until the vegetables are tender, approximately 40 minutes. Remove from heat, add parsley and lemon juice. Season with kosher salt.

There's nothing like making a pot of vegetable soup. Given my background, I suggest using chicken broth. It smells and tastes like what my grandmothers made.

Sun sets, sit down with others ...
enjoy a sumptuous meal.

DINNER

Cauliflower, Carrot & Cashew Soup
(3-4 servings)

2 tbsp coconut oil
1 medium onion, chopped
1 fresh ginger, grated
1 tsp fresh turmeric, grated
1 1/2 cups raw whole cashews, soaked 6 hours
1 small head cauliflower, broken into pieces
1 large carrot, chopped
1/2 cup coconut milk
salt & pepper to taste

Lightly saute onion, carrot, ginger, turmeric in
coconut oil, until the carrot softens a little.

Add soaked cashews and cauliflower.
Add water to 1/8 inch below cauliflower level.
Simmer until cauliflower and carrot are just soft.

Add coconut milk, salt & pepper, and blend thoroughly.
Serve immediately.

Tastes are made, not born.
A Tramp Abroad, Mark Twain

Tex-Mex Chili (3 servings)

1 tbsp extra-virgin olive oil
1/2 tbsp chili powder
1/2 tsp ground cumin
1/2 lb grass-fed beef or substitute, finely chopped
1/4 cup fresh cilantro, chopped
1/4 cup sweet onion, finely chopped
1/2 15-ounce can black beans
1/2 15-ounce can pinto beans
1/3 clove garlic, minced
1/2 cup fresh tomatoes with green chilies
1/2 cup shredded cheddar cheese (optional)

Heat the olive oil in a large pot with lid, over medium heat.
Add the beef and cook for 5 minutes.

Add the onion, garlic, chili powder, and cumin.
Cook over medium-low heat for 6 minutes.

Add the beans, with their liquid, and the tomatoes.

Continue cooking, covered, on low heat for 30 minutes.
Sprinkle with cheese, if desired.

A locally brewed beer, cider, or favorite wine
compliments this meal. Try a sparkling water
for a non-alcoholic option.

Lentils with Red Onions & Rice
(2 servings)

1 cup sprouted brown lentils
2 to 3 cups water
1 vegetable bouillon cube
1 red onion, thinly sliced
1 tbsp butter substitute
3 cloves garlic, minced
1/2 tsp red pepper flakes
1 cup fresh parsley, chopped
1/2 cup olive oil
1 tsp salt
1/2 tsp black pepper
1 package of your favorite rice

Cook one cup dry rice according to package instructions.

Bring lentils to boil in water. Simmer until soft and the water has evaporated. Add the bouillon cube and stir. Keep warm.

In large skillet, put the onions slices into butter substitute and simmer 15-20 minutes. Stir often.

Add the garlic, salt, pepper, and chili flakes to the onions. Add lentils and stir. Add parsley and olive oil.

Add fresh diced tomato or spinach and heat before serving over rice.

Let's honor the Polish proverb,
as we introduce this meal from the sea:

Fish to taste right must swim three times:
in water, in butter, and in wine.

Baked Salmon (2 servings)

2 salmon fillets
1/4 cup melted butter substitute
1/3 cup lemon juice
1/4 cup white wine
1 tsp Worcestershire sauce
2 tsp seasoning salt
black pepper to taste

Rinse the salmon fillets and pat dry.

In a small bowl whisk together the lemon juice,
melted butter substitute, wine and Worcestershire sauce.
Season with salt and black pepper to taste (and sneeze).

Pour this mixture into a shallow 9-inch baking dish.
Add in salmon steaks; turn to coat.
Cover and chill for 30 minutes.

Heat oven to 400 degrees F. Bake for 10 minutes.

Remove from oven and spoon the sauce over the fish.
Bake for another 10 minutes until the fish flakes.

Enjoy with a glass of Sauvignon blanc,
ideally from New Zealand.

Baked Spaghetti (3 servings)

Ingredients:
1 package gluten-free thin spaghetti noodles
  (or zucchini noodles)
1/2 lb ground beef, or substitute
1/2 tsp minced garlic
1 13-ounce can spaghetti sauce
1 cup shredded cheddar cheese, or substitute
1/2 tbsp oregano

Preheat oven to 350 degrees F.

Cook spaghetti in boiling water; drain.

Brown ground beef and garlic over medium heat;
drain fat. Combine ground beef, spaghetti sauce,
and oregano.

Place half the noodles in bottom of a greased dish.
Add half the spaghetti sauce mix and half of the cheese.
Repeat the process twice, adding the remaining cheese.

Bake for 30 minutes.

Red or rosé wine goes well with this meal.

Meatloaf (3 servings)

3/4 lb lean ground beef or tempeh
1/2 cup crushed crackers
1/2 cup onion, chopped
1 egg
1/4 cup almond (or coconut) milk
1/4 cup catsup
1/2 tbsp Worcestershire sauce

Preheat oven to 350 degrees F.

In a large bowl, combine beef, crackers, onion,
egg, milk, 1/8 cup catsup, Worcestershire sauce,
salt, and pepper.

In a small baking pan, shape the mixture into a loaf.
Spread the remaining catsup over top.
Cover and bake for 30 minutes.

Bake, uncovered, for 30 more minutes.

A red wine is called for with this hearty dish.

Good food ends with good talk.
Geoffrey Neighbor

To be enjoyed between meals or late at night.
Nibble ... set limits.

Healthy Desserts and Snacks

Sliced ripe mango or papaya, with a squeeze
of fresh lemon on top;

Sliced carrots, bell pepper, or celery with hummus;

A small box of organic seedless raisins;

A handful of organic roasted & salted almonds,
cashews, pistachios, or macadamia nuts;

Sliced banana, pear, apple, plum, or kiwi;

Granola bar of your choice;
    (I recommend Raw Revolution because it's the best.
    Try the Chocolate Crave, and you'll see what I mean.)

1 ounce dark chocolate (necessitates setting limits);

1 cup organic applesauce;
    (Try buying apples in season, and make this sauce
    yourself. It's a real treat)

1 cup of your favorite organic trail-mix;

Small bag of freshly made organic popcorn,
add salt and coconut butter to taste.

ABOUT THE AUTHOR

David H. Rosen is a physician, psychiatrist, and Jungian analyst. His interests include: finding meaning in suffering; spirituality as it relates to healing; dreams; and all kinds of creativity, especially visual art and haiku.

David is the author and co-author of over fifteen books, ranging from a children's coloring book and a memoir, to his many medical works. His next project concerns the beginnings of Opal Whiteley.

Currently living in Eugene, Oregon, with his wife Lanara and their rescued Akita named Suki, David walks, paints, sees analytic patients, and leads a dream group.

David is a standup comedian and uses the performance name, "Dr Nada."

Dr Nada has decided that if this cookbook doesn't sell, he will eat it (while his lovely wife Lanara laughs out loud).

ALSO FROM ROSENBERRY BOOKS AND WIPF & STOCK:
800.723.0336 // 541.344.1528

The Tao of Elvis, David H. Rosen, MD, illus. Diane Katz

"Magnificent ... Truly a work of art. It brings to mind the inspired illuminated manuscripts of the Middle Ages." — Sue Monk Kidd, author of *The Secret Life of Bees*. In a most readable fashion, Rosen illuminates the inner Elvis and the myth of Elvis. Sumptuously designed and illlustrated.

Lost in the Long White Cloud, David H. Rosen, MD

A cinematic and astonishingly honest adventure story, Rosen's memoir takes us all over the map. In Greece, David lays awake under the stars with lovely Lolly and decides to become a fisherman. He pays a Parisian prostitute just to listen to her story, which deeply informs the future Jungian psychiatrist. Later, Dr Rosen will coin the term "egocide" and publish his magnum opus.

ABOUT THE ARTIST

Diane Katz uses a high-energy drawing technique employing creamy blocks of beeswax crayons. The result is a cross between printing, drawing and monument rubbing in which hidden images magically reveal themselves on the surface of the paper. Diane's work has been seen at museums such as the Metropolitan Museum of Art, the Smithsonian, the Chicago Institute of Art, and the Washington National Cathedral.

Other books that include Diane's artwork are:
Time, Love and Licorice and *The Tao of Elvis* by Dr Rosen;
On All My Holy Mountain: *A Modern Fraktur*;
Apples Dipped in Honey: a Jewish ABC;
The Story-Letters from Appletta Tooth Fairy.

Once employed as a natural food store produce buyer, Diane now lives with her husband in the woods of North Carolina. She cooks and preserves local, organic foods. She also soaks and dries quantities of almonds purchased directly from farmers in California, as well as pumpkin seeds from farmers in David Rosen's own Oregon.

Time, Love and Licorice:
A Healing Coloring Storybook
by David H. Rosen, MD

The attic is a wondrous place. It is a place to fix things: Dad's workshop is there, and Henry's special corner, which hides his secret supply of building blocks. When his soldier father comes back changed, Henry's fantastic block towers are threatened by Dad's sudden outbursts.

But in the attic inspirations come, and repairs of all kinds are made...

The drawings of Henry's optimistic, creative and imaginative world create a safe space in which children and families can face the disruptions of Post-Traumatic Stress Disorder (PTSD).